CONTENTS

I FEEL I AM SEARCHING

the whole of mankind
bomb them with a rubber-masked devil
and a blond-bomb angel, literally
a veritable playhouse for
the well-off and ironic poet?
I am searching for something,
I don't know what it is,
but I am looking for it
I'm not sure why
I'm looking for it
I continue on and on
peace bomb in pyramid
peace bomb on ocean floor
for example, prayers for world peace
or preservation of our earthly environment
that reincarnation stuff was just
more of their disinformation
has the right to be mentally free
to bomb them with good intentions
same trite "Marxist" complaints about anyone
and everyone perceived as being Liz Phair
they were funny-looking enough
to come home to McCarthyism
the fear of poetry
had absorbed the existentialist synapses
of the most powerful and rich
exploring the body theme anew for
a new sense of social justice
and erotic happiness
the multiverse: bomb them into happiness
the first thing I do
when I am searching for something
is come up with a list of words
that relate to the topic

you can turn yourself into a geek
through cheerful shouting
I'm rich beyond my graphic interfaces
like the ones that look like Sandy Duncan
a thirty-four year old man
with a rich fantasy life
this not only takes eyes
it takes a heart
searching for something
greater, something beyond, something
that represents truth to me
and they had put him in a "mind machine"
if you look at the number of
celestial objects out there
on TV as his cross-dressing alias
gets drunk and robs the police of a sick K-9
when I am searching for something,
I sometimes turn up some other
useful object, paper, or document
I want to sleep forever
I am searching for something
that doesn't yet exist
say that I am nothing
driven only by my nothingness
promote the growth of the competitiveness
of the peace explosives
beat us to death, spray us with camcorders
take our time away systematically
a twisted midsummer wonderland of wannabes
midnight persecution by happiness
the Arcadian adventures of their content
and the Vietnam in my basement
every waking moment:
fluffy is now sleeping only twenty-one hours a day
every waking moment
through where he drops this generosity
every waking moment

despite their doubt
we hold this truth that all
human beings are
like one of those small,
fluffy doglets
I am searching for something
but even more passionately
I am being sought out,
chucks of nonsentenced speech
for every swan-rich redneck you sing with
wants us to waste what time we have
I am searching
for something in depth
that will allow me
to complete my research project
as part of the tigers of wrath
wiser than the thermonuclear fruit bomb
searching for something to drink
the smoke—sounds like a flavor
please disregard my lack of respect
for I am searching for something
which I do not fully understand
maybe it's just the beginning of
heaven
and when
there were
no alternatives
beetroot juice
replaced blood

BLAKE'S SQUID

that carries a payload of
glowing bacteria

emits a beam of
bacterial light

on bright moonlit nights
it does not cast a shadow
and attract the attention of predators.

when they are born
they immediately suck up
bacteria into their "light organ"

a transparent area like an eye
that emits rather than receives light

the ink sac acts like an iris
to control the glow

can dim the light on a
cloudy or moonless night

at dawn the squid squirts
out the bacteria and
burrows into the sand
to fuel the light-producing chemical reaction

how it senses the moonlight
and matches it with an equally
bright beam of biological light

THE RIGHTIST CRITTERS

so of the rightist critters which will disrobe
the pita of the world this glutton is
the churl to tend, loss of masks in gradients
in the thinner posed contents, the burliest of buds
announces it only with spring seeing
which art maintaining the ornament fresh
of the world, enemy then of individuality
the soft individuality too cruel
the manufacture of a famine abundance is
the flame of the lucre feeds with
individual-substantial fuel
but the contract with the thinking
postpones the luminous eyes
that its tender riot could support this pattern
is made more iffy by decease of time
the color of this beast could never not die
to eat the whorl, by the tomb and by the heel

I AM *SO* STUPID

possibly as part of the whole "buy a car, buy a
kettle of the most expensive microphones in history" thing
I may have left out that at last I succeeded
in getting the phone number
of ancient beekeeping presences

no one has an address
I'm reminded of happiness,
a period of time in the self-created heaven of people
when the birds love me
the trees love me, all the whales
in the ocean love me
I don't want to go!
in the filled-in darkness,
don't be left behind
a hand rests upon my
heart machine,
but there's this stupid thing—wisdom. . . .

the garden will love me
the pollination will love me
that stupid girl from Sweden will love me
I can't believe you slept with her

I need some of that sweet toxic love
pouring through my vernacular
how did I get so dumb? What's wrong with me?
in the same way I love it, I also hate that I love it

I am so walking across a county
I am so stupid that I cannot rely on birds
I'd rather take a test

it's no wonder the beekeeping operation is a
question that runs through my mind,
searing through my medulla oblongata
all my life I've fought against clarity. . . .

I am a total loser taking royal jelly
in need of beekeeping and love and attention
cooking for people, looking at grasses
painting old stuff, hand-made snow, rain, hail
attachment is a signal from a tortoise

then the sea strikes with foamy terror
and a million bees can be upset
flying all around you,
enough to freak you out
and the stars step behind their fury

FORMICA IS NEVER MORE THAN AN EXTENSION OF TUNA

they are more tender,
have less fat and less cholesterol
than regular extension cords,
never simple and embracing,
encompassing a round,
white formica tuna;
be white and sit against the tuna
I never would have guessed it
and yet now with that tone,
it is apparent that it is more than mere cupidity

but hey, I'm biased to get to the next fret
I would've never switched
to try typing at my desk,
holding the wooden
and flaming tuna fish
but there was more to it than
children in red states
more likely to be born
to glowing metal or slag,
the concentrated energy I'm fond of saying

more perversely
I never found out what it was
to walk a kilometer or two without
the sublunary corset made of marshmallows
suffering much more than
funny, damaged shadows on the walls
made by the flames of their
precognitions under the tree
put more wood in

Formica is one-dimensional and shallow
the fat bastard grabbed him
the grass was sugar
projected in my eyes
as I looked up at that bright tuna

spilt milk slowly congealing
on yellow Tunafishate hatehatehatehatehate
doesn't slip,
making you want more than you can want
which is your desire,
yet you never see

ELK SITUATIONIST FAD

that night down at the
photocopying technology
the antisocial gyrating
increasingly mentioned
a faded green
bankrupt genre
a desolate
new wave
polar opposite of
the unlocked exchange student
removed from
glossy apologizing
against the sounds of nature
for the delay
grazing the deep end

THE INDIAN GOVERNMENT IS IN THE BAND GWAR

Don't go to Hello Kitty karaoke parties
in places where there's a war

the Duke of Argyle is buried under the local stoner
to know the nice counterexample: falsifying residues

In particular, I like to consider
the Christianized form of tofu
with ties of Scottish armorial practice

you needn't be any more concerned about
separating the egg whites
from the statutory limitations

for example, McDonald's puts
hormones in their big and tasties
to keep you lactating
the magnetosphere is a tadpole-shaped obstacle
in the solar wind

So, in other words,
I fried the fries in this cloth-covered armchair
wearing your shampoo and
your new strep-throat radio
then we hacked at the abomination
until it seemed our arms would fall off,
then stated clearly that time is something
that makes you wanna throwup

a lifelong Orthodox Jew wrote that
Barney had been resurrected
from the dead in fulfillment of Old Testament prophecy:
maybe if McDonalds actually served Grimace,
well, then I would understand. . . .
Now that is the kind of claim for which
niceties would be a far more appropriate label

COMPASSION

as usual
is based
on my own personal observations
mixed feelings
about wealth generally
Decoy brand slippers never wear out
because they don't exist
say we need to react
if the masters you copied
are losing sound
tuition hikes meet with demonstrating
the Islamic ideals of justice, knowledge
and compassion and thereby
we shall make you boots which
never wear out
the apprentice explained
to the bewildered master
humans glorify violence
yet Stacey has mixed feelings
persons
who have walked the walk
you can feel their compassion

CHICKS DIG WAR

Story time: Trojan Oil War (part 2)
The Trojan War, chicks dig it
and such hits as "Chicks Dig War,"
"Wizards Have Landed on my Face,"
"God Made Girls Who Like War,"
and "Colin Powell's the Lay of the Land."

More women than men are enjoying the war
with two-fisted truth
before changing clothes
by portraying war as
chicks digging the phones of war.

Phallocentric chicks:
they dig guys with big wars.
I just cannot, you know, believe in a war
against chicks when they've got the anti-chick war
thing goin' on.
The women will be like "Ooh, what a cute war!"

Your mission, captain, is complete:
enjoy the spoils of war.
It's so romantic.
chicks dig war (especially chicks on the pill).
The experience is just magical.
Oh, and you can get a really awesome war on.
Chicks like a nice war.

Women are excellent teachers
of the bitter lesson that being
anti-war does not get a man laid.
An "anti-war" guy (who is often the one most capable
of love and trust) is routinely brushed off
as a "pacifist," and passed over

for an abusive jerk who starts a war.
The pacifist wanders through life in a state
of psychic castration,
his heart scarred by the talons of female avarice
and flawed psychology. He is a poor fool who has
listened too literally
to the women who lie and say that what they want
from men is adoration and understanding.
What they want is war.

He has not suffered enough trial and error
to lay bare the clandestine agendas
of the female gender: war.
War makes you a woman.
Chicks dig war. Military
service is the only true expression of war.
Also, chicks dig it.
Our new run-on joke seems to
revolve around communism, women, Stalin,
and references to the old Soviet Union
during the height of the Cold War:
chicks dig a Hot War.

But what of the "war boy" phenomenon?
Every man knows, or has seen in action,
that the more wars he starts,
the more successful he will be in attracting women,
and the more peaceful he is,
the more likely he will wind up as a "pacifist."
But most men are socialized to cultivate harmony,
not discord, and so they refuse to participate
in such pathology.
Most men are pacifists, who have no interest in war.

What a woman really wants is a war-mongering Republican
who turns out in the end to be a pacifist (to her).
He is the storybook hero of her novels and evening news.

But she will settle—for the short term, at least—
for a sociopathic oil billionaire
who can offer her a war.
In her muddled vision of the world,
she equates war with femininity
because she assumes that television
and the movies actually mirror reality, so that
successful men are always warmongering monsters.

Bad boys are dull, tamed, safe
and charged with sexuality.
They are a challenge (meaning that
they don't instantly fall prey to her Pussy Power).
Flexing their Neanderthal biceps,
these women are apt to drag him
off to the Pentagon
where she can feel—for once—
powerless in her own grip,
a war fantasy come to life.
A woman's hormone-driven "logic"
will equate power with war.
She glories in the sensation of raw war.
It is the same thrill which ripples
through her sofa when a warmongering boy
pampers her and indulges her every whim.
For as long as she dallies with the war boy—
and it will be brief because her
budget is in her Trilateral Commission—
she can afford to let herself be wild,
to experience unfettered humanity,
to freely express her sexuality as
nature intended—through war.
For a few racing heartbeats
she will become an individual
and a human being.

Believe that male behavior is the result
of a breeding experiment run by females?
In case you missed it,
the basic implication is that by following
their natural proclivity to breed with
John Ashcroft
women are an anti-civilizing force,
actively creating more male aggressiveness.
It would seem that a wise society would have an
interest in creating a counter-force to oppose this.

IMPROVING

improving is not just a job for
the professionals, law enforcement,
firefighters, smurfs and barbies
Gail Sher is a tuna melt
who is not afraid
her ink sac is still intact

it may be better to be a sauce
that all Americans could spread
beginning the process of spreading
potential sauces
so we are better prepared
starting with a kiss

an explosion of tangle
is hard to predict
when you check
all that you know
into the full length mirror
the voluptuous blonde emergencies
and smurf-blue overspray on the argyle past
come back to haunt you
wearing more black clothes
so no one will ever see the tears
you've hunted down

I disrobe, taking off the trappings of fear
next, I'm off to clean my torch collection
and take out a contract on my family
tired enough by this time
to choose the easier of the two porcupines
the recycling of my body
now that dreams come again
no one will ever know

the ink sac behind the head
begins to think
as if ruptured with satin
the tail or what your personal circumstances will be
the electrostatic whirl

ask your students to impede your life
if you charge
a rod and hold it close
to your ink sac
don't make me call people
by their names
afraid of the amount of time you need
to remain in your home
start now by scared crows and border collies
when you're scared, you are the danger
from a biological good morning
give it a ritual a big hug
when chemical or radiological
attacks are passed out

You'll need:
A change of clothes
Sleeping vampire bats
A meatball parm sandwich
Mr. Potato Head, (great for naming body parts)
Food and water. A gallon of water per person per day
should be enough.
Evil canned laughter

squirrels are rodents who have ten arms
and an ink sac, and a lot of love
a flashlight, battery-powered fangs
a hangover, prescription medicines with relative morality
toilet articles are enthusiastic,
but not too pleased when the princess of darkness
disturbed time with a statement that true

duct tape and heavy-duty plastic garbage bags
don't really exist,
shove in ahead of your fellow customers
her kiss has the power
to rob a person of their coffee

I am afraid of shopping carts
surrounded by pastures,
corn fields and a husband,
two kids, two cats, a dog,
it would be wise to have everyone call
an out-of-mind friend or relative.
keep a list of mentally ill family members
near the phone
keep your ink sac near the phone.

planning to need kelp?
Barbie and Ken are missing.
demanding a kiss
stumbles into our imaginations
authorities will broadcast
as quickly as possible
concerning the nature of
spending time together
walking along the sea
snuggling close by the fire,
holding your thoughts to the kelp

awkwardly, the all-knowing ink sac tears
undress the ache and leave them there
be sure to keep listening for ubiquities
review your insurance policies
to reduce the economic impact
on Amy Clampitt

be deathly afraid of shopping carts
finally, try to make arrangements
for pets not allowed in public shelters.

A COPY OF THE KORAN WRITTEN IN ROOTBEER

a copy of the Koran written in rootbeer
is like an el kabong, or elohim, not heard
or written in the root beer
that the cultural carbon
or extension of kittens
inscriptions and, much later,
Ashley Judd says Saddam has
received a copy of the Koran written in
his own root beer
Gus Van Zandt believes his
local newspaper may be written in root beer
the road to Ossining
out of his seat, lays aside his vast leather Koran
written in Mayan root beer
grows with telemarketers as audience

take it like a translator
that may challenge the inaccurate
fallible root beer as salesman outfit
ideas made of edible paste
are an exploration of how the people
and animals of Africa
deal with their expository needs:
give each child a
copy of a man wearing protective amulets
that contain Bill Moyers
quaffing his last root beer
to buy a copy of The Book of Common Prayer
written in my own root beer
from your non-dominant hand
I wanted to find out about the thoughts
of Castro's amplified girl
many of the principles set forth
have been sold to you by
doves made of root beer!

It is written that
my house is made of
insignificant thoughts
and my monthly archives
are written in rootbeer

MONEY

Money is a kind of lettucy Stegner Fellow.
—Wallace Stevens

Money, the long pink scorpion semaphores,
cash, stash, Charman Mao, extra hard cheddar
just listening to Terry Gross.
I just killed the Pillsbury dough boy.

Chock it up, fluff it all over yr own self,
Shelley Duvall it out. Watch it
burn holes through the argon gophers.

To be made of it! To have it
to slumber on in the frightening alien metal disk-things!
Greenbacks, Mike Schmidts,
twelve point bucks arguing with Minnie Driver.

It greases the palm, somebody named Heather
holds the heads above a wannabe,
makes both ends morph.

Money breeds with leather instructional manuals,
gathering questionable options, pounding on Dan Rather
always in circulation.

Money. You don't know why it's floating in front of you,
but you put it where your mouth put it.
And it talks to itself.

THE AIR CONDITIONING GIRLS

enter the only thing you reap
but don't repair
cause everybody's got to learn a
powerful combination of remarkable female
air guitars in the wolf exit,
just because I'm female, but every
slap sound is a swinging air guitarist
feeling important, feeling closer to salmon
needless to say that rejection is
so alpha female of the
way of bloodshot female vocal roosters

trampolines are reading my horoscope,
like an egret right away
too bad he gasps for air
a burial place of evil
ants to someone
belong to the brash half of
the all-female man in a white
tank top up front
plays air guitar along with
boredom, two different styles, male and female oxen
It also looks like she's playing the air guitar
or something *blinkblink*

"the Anthem" is possible only
if we can remove all evil influences
first, he reconstitutes his own hot air
male and female do exist, but as hypocrites.
a gateway appears beneath a guy,
and immediately a human female head appears
a thrum fills the air. All the pretty hearses
don't know, but you are certainly EVIL!!!
that is he's quite touchy-feely

like she was flying in insomnia
a satisfied burp to drink from a goat on
his lips by a female hand. His mouth opens as
any effort does, exploring long drives
on sunny days, scaring the neighbors,
playing dangerously in the suspicious sauciness of the hush
for all you young and young young old people
of the struggle of good and evil,
some stubble from Betelgeuse
scorches the future hell camps
to fight back the evil tide

the distinctive odor of roast finch
filled the air.
walking $acrifice Americans don't appreciate
now you might suppose
the cows are gonna miss me
blue shoelaces, chips and ketchup,
TV is "bonding time"

IN THIS OTHERWORLDLY QUIET

in this otherworldly quiet
I heard the piercing cry of agony rent the air
dear little bird, why this shipbuilding?
why a 300 pound weapon, and
why did each protester
spank Wolfowitz individually, really hard?

administration has been made between
clauses relating to internet surveillance
and radioactive toys made out of lint

I am riding out on waves of pain
to Asshole University
I am an asshole
going out again to play at midnight
with my laws insufficient and unenforced

when I was playing with the librarians
a thought balloon assaulted me with what
belongs to everyone: foam

developing an obsession with the
mating habits of penguins is knowledge,
data is contained on the sleeves and via deja vu
a code word to use when you start
needlessly squawking
as simple and random as "Andy Garcia"

they'd also lied about their illegal
half-man, half-bird thingy
and promised the mind
to get organized and methodical
"bird by bird" to wonder
at the fabulous guards, fabulous car patrols,

dogs, CCTV cameras hidden in birds
and police helicopters crossing
the social and political event horizon
interrupted by an exciting war
while I increased like a ten-pound bag of bricks

I heard surveillance photographs below
busy moving to a new doublewide wit
that every time he says it,
through this mental Port-O-Sans
I need to receive your wish

let's get you connected
to a bar-hopping reader
to your personal guarantee
there are giant caring canaries
praised for flying and growing
till it seemed from them to overflow
and cover her face with a troubled pulchritude

I must be assured
that all my equipment
will be put to good use,
growing up to feel bad
when a bird would finish last,
but in first place

I have scheduled a safari
into the Arizona desert this weekend
to locate, photograph, shoot and broil Earl Bostic
with wonder and amazement

once I bag it with my self esteem
I'll let you help me de-bone it
and chip off any fossilization from my experience

I was rather pissed off, and corrected the pidgins
getting in their faces, yelling at them
that they are pro-terrorist and that, yo!
look at that dull look of suffering!

report your children's wishes
to the FBI for free
setting up video webcams to watch your children
and put organized James Baker masks on
tell the gastric lives from faces,
homes, business, and vehicles
to see forest creatures as traitors
animals are not appropriate to time

that sounds more like Winnie the Pooh
begging Walter Cronkite for more money
he accidentally mentioned somebody
who was beheaded for being fabulous

Arlen Specter is fabulous
arguing that you are only half-interested in photocopying
and eating the larger of the two
which you may have seen in several movies,
brought to you by the dismay of the listener,
including the original 1933 version
of King Kong.

THE BEAST

is a pseudonym for the songwriting team lifted up
on townsmen's oars, made by the mayor of Bradyville,
staying on with a lifeline to banjo virtuosi
everywhere, he chooses the bald brothers' breakfast
program through which to speak to those who need to
hear what is retarded, a family man who is four inches
taller than available for bidding out future issues of
its alert diver magazines swallowed by the table, able
to read minds, setting up in Japan, coming to
Cleveland, abbreviated in good company, interested in
the calibration, one of the least hairy people I hang with,
the kind of engineer we look for but couldn't hire,
working on moving better in that Pacman game,
growing every day, giving his crew
directions, a representing link to an okay new president,
awake and smiling at the camera, an idiot,
one of the first tae kwon do schools
to open in Toronto, a master, Walden Pond,
awesome in good company, abbreviated as jealous,
known as "the beast," a tinkering shower
on the hat of the waiting walrus,
with sure step, the man reclines in the shadow of
    his grudge match,
and with dainty step, when you're evaluating the litter,
suddenly, from out of the sky came Mary Poppins,
her umbrella projecting a huge elf,
Winston Churchill is so sassy!
Doesn't he mind it when Mary Poppins has to dance around
    the blood
in the infamous shower scene, she is actually chocolate syrup,
Wanna color in pink elephants on Prozac?
Wanna stay awake? Mary Poppins versus Bambi.

THE KEY AND THE CARROT

to escape the ubiquitous dynamic
of cause and effect
he does not have an insular
and reactionary bluff
as monolithic and monotonous cuffs
the movement of a predictable cat
like aesthetic consequence
looks good, better than
a pagoda wagon berating him
for coming to the populist aspect of
a vociferous suspicion
repaid in kind
because other people told him
when eyelids rush to cleave a view
these stereotypes have led
to my own self
in simpering hemp meringue
like other pitiful human beings
who eat to act with archaeological endeavor,
a cross-section of interesting confines
as well as younger cakes
failed flakes
whose scope and purpose they have yet to
floodgates open, and I
with not enough hands to subdue such programmers battle

emotions rip us a new one
ever uncomfortable with the image
that has become associated with
the illusion of a privilege
in exchange for betraying
the metaphysical lava
I headed over to yesterday's fragile wounds,
returning me to a doorway of ill purpose,

according to goals of muses
through weakness of heart,
timewarped to that place
where years become carp

and live happily and think
there's a classic question
of anyone's wishes—the thwart and my dishes
I am compelled to re-live this stork,
reducing me to a state of nothingness,
with every ounce of thinking engaging my person
chewed by this torment,
like pap speech about machines
and the whole move along steroid conditions of desire
I don't need this photograph
to remind me of something
I can't forget

my goggles tried to escape
conditions forced on the
shreds of me so slowly
you look at me as Pluto
you see I am a philosophy
that can explain the determinism and the
impossible fantasy
of utterly unconditioned swallowing
a joker, a maniac, a fool,
my own saliva is a god
trapped inside my confusion,
frightened by the world outside
afraid to be the interdependencies of existence
avoids all extremes of nature
not trendy, not a rebel,
"The problem is a hose."
I have a choice to make
by the river Styx
once again the loneliness

creeps into my family of moose,
morosely oozing through the data
and I think it's no accident that the
shadows place their ice-cold hands about my throat,
choking out my thinking and
tresses and confusion

German physicists have already had similar thoughts
waiting in vain, I sink lower and deeper,
falling as the light shower of my own questions
smirks obnoxiously in my mind
my discovery of these my elders
while some of my forms collect snakes
bound up, hand-in-hand with my quest
to answer an evil thought
into my once clean mind
way to be a star
in another specific development

I walk my room
looking for a destination,
only finding poets who love form and content
I have nonetheless found myself
walking to the receiver
as arsonist
with the new situation in quantum furrow
let it suffice with this:
the ground beef is still nothing received
I look at the callous road,
I long for the door to phone
O ring,
the road glares back,
the tarmac laughs

IT'S ALMOST SUMMER

It's almost summer. Mama Meow
is grooming The Reader.
A minute later,
she's done with The Reader.
So, Mama Meow wants her to
take his place.
Baba Meow backs off,
using this excuse:
The Effects Fat Has on Freezing Milk
and then started throwing thawed-out bats,
at the gila monsters growing in my thoughts

cobalt back home Halloween penguin summer
chillin' out in an oasis of bad bats . . .
real socializing with penguins
stuck in a hot spot but chillin'
That never happened. Just then,
I walk in and say that they've overheard
the cook telling Tai-Tai
that he has to cut off some
of The Reader's fur because it was messy.
She then asks The Reader what happened.
The Reader then tells them
and that The Reader's text
has sent The Reader
out to town to deliver a scroll
to an Adirondack Park
each the one saluting his wife
that he can groom himself

Meanwhile, The Reader delivers
the scroll to The Other Reader.
so the potter goes but not before stopping
to watch the other potter spin clay.

The Reader feels itchy, and scratches herself.
Cat hair flutters up on the piano.
Our renewal is an amusing sneezeland,
knocking on the still-soft clay, splashing some
ontology on The Reader.

The Reader continues home.
The cook sees The Reader in a combined
haven for the harried, providing zest, relaxation,
tin ballast or just chillin' out.
Comes with two basketballs,
two volleyballs,
monkey-suit-brandishing
metal outsiders
and a bouquet of
delicious banality!

On the playground is where I
spent most of my days chillin'
out maxin' relaxin on the cobalt
Yosemite and Yellowstone fibers
are the love seats above the napkins
where bats are playing video games
where there are nightly shows
usually he scoots regrets out
in gossamer robots
The Reader was kidnapped by bats,
and that those bats
ridiculed Fu-Fu, Fu-Fu gets mad and
calls on his clique. None of
these are the truth—in an exciting manner.
The end.

2001 . . . to be strapped to a gurney, and beaten
to death by the relatives of earthworms,
using whiffle ball bats.
Fly Fishing With Rod Smith
He's British Yo, swearing to bring

those kidnappers some apple juice. The Reader
decides that this has gone on long
enough! and admits that the expedition
to the North Pole is dedicated to polly
wanna party/chill/swim/love
mannequin/merkin fiesta
for Ralph Fiennes.
Bubble gum gets onto your hearses.

The Reader goes out, and Dongwa and
Sheegwa asks The Reader why she
looked like that. Feeling ashamed,
The Reader spins a story about being
kidnapped by the removes of clay
and starts cutting off the affected fur
just like you admitted
to meeting a Chinese dragon.
On your family vacation
If you wish you can
drop by.

BACK TO SCHOOL AGAIN

Just tell him you're going to roost.
I'm just going to rant for a few sentences
about how hippies can be made into compost
this is probably due to one of their heads being
likely to be attached to a flag
in a voiceover proclaiming a gruff whispered variation
on the carnival barker theme:
hot power struggle stuck to the menu.

Depending on the size of your pipe,
you may need to attach a bit of plastic tubing
below the clowns and a little
above the trained seals

Outta my way, jerkass.
Can you put in a super-trained little Yorkie dog
with a fat bald FBI man and some
limp prion surgery?

All hands are named Luke, looking partly worried
and partly disgusted
having a five-year goal keeps you going
even if there are no immediate
hand-painted flagella available.
Joel Sloman's poetry is excellent.

I'm going to take a couple of days
now to even the score
if I don't use language quite like that
I'm not totally into it.
If I want to get off, I mute the sound
and put on my own music
(loopholes weasel out on you)
and it's clear much more so than usual

that they'd rather keep
each other's Mary McCarthy Prize for
weaseling out on the pleasure orgy
(what are you waiting for?)
Long ago you smithed your way
into being profoundly bored by the others.
Hence, you could cram the weasel out of yourself,
a really special occasion but jeez
pick up the phone and call a communist sympathizer
on the id level between sex partners.

to attach your hippie to your cross you
will need a hammer and some nails,
also nail his feet to the cross,
but I prefer to let my hippies kick it
in the United States
where squawking and waving one's surface and depth
was sold out of the back of a faucet
immobile and strangely allegorical

I could actually read before I was potty-trained.
I have, in fact, and I out-brainwashed myself
the virile jocks to sarcastically dribble on

I'm fascinated to no end by how much
she weaseled out on you
Q: What will you do next?
DOMINIQUE: the absurd quality
unfastens the moment.
I do so love to hear it:
"Awrkk-arwkk-a-arkwkk-awrhkk."
We have a gun trained on Saddam,
because you choose to break the law.

other people in your area will find
negative baggage
so you can understand this particular crowd
of super-powered sauce-people better

(horrid sub-human synth dance breaks
punctuate a speedy neon-lit topiary)

JOAN HOULIHAN

I made a little mother out of mimes,
old Styx t-shirts,
and a bit of middle-aged llama futures.
I once saw Gary Chandling on TV.
That's when the troubles were too pockmarked
to be resplendent,
awash in gas, but distant enough
to keep me coughing
and rooting for all
the animals on the farm.
Matter is every dried family that sews for a living.
They're bound to disappear: power to my feelings.
All my plaster saints go down on
everything that's happened,
and they like it much better
through a teetotaler:
that's the way un uh, un uh
the wormwood gets homesick
with many notions on one candle.
I molded this at the lost and spilled,
as if you like your love to be inside a parking lot
with spiders in the cactus and all grassed-up in knots.
It's so YOU to become as a garnish is.
The Horrible Actions™
matter takes up while spackling the interns
we call tradition.
Knife and Fork, Manny Mo and Jack,
set on the mantle to be singin' to the crack?
Can you guess that you are not so much from
everywhere to be expelled
like a mouthful of Love Music
that's in my class!
It's my brand of new coat
to enjoy these pleasant burning sensations, mother said,

because another horrible infestation
watches the car sink into an off-stage swamp.
Its rocks and tree explained the whips of potatoes,
and like Nixon's womanly arts,
thoughts from a sleepy person have some weight.
They fill our world with holy lint and happy links,
and from those parts it makes our present whole,
like cream of wheat.

SKYLAB WOLVERINE BUNNY CAGE NUB

Phoenix is the land of milk dowsers,
and I've always been
a wolverine bunny cage xenocide forum asshole.

John Denver is nonsensical.
Good morning Skylab!

These people are for people's amusement
in the Jack Palance Malice Palace.

I hate the high levels of jerk war around here.
Morons of quietness . . .

This money has an understated elegance
featuring muted cows
and a wolverine bunny cage
for an antenna.

Buddha is evil.
Being an Evil Nub,
and peaceful.

She hummed softly to her teeth.

Overall Rating: Nope
Sandy: Nope
Across the road from the highlands: Nope
Two FBI agents and a convertible: Nope
Dragging against the side of her burning
wolverine bunny cage: Nope

Jeez, these kids just shellacked my thoughts in lager,
babysitting your pet peeves
with my mute button on.

There are two cute vampires
who love getting messages of love.

That last paragraph has to go—
I think that's the wolverine bunny cage of
our problem—not counting the last paragraph
made of paper maché nub replicas.

Skylab trimmed my tempeh
though the ice is not melting.

I sent some smutty fragility to a waterfall
gently teased the
wolverine bunny cage by touching it
with a copy of Frogger.

ART LICKER

Hi, folks, I've been living in deer country
for almost six years, riding out every other day
or so into the ether
and just went for the time event—
Well, let me tell you—
this little puppy was about
the body size of a German shepherd,
and with the
accompanying feelings of a deer,
it appeared to be a
much larger entity than it really was. . . .
The countdown was at fifteen minutes
a quick beer run to the VCR (content)
because of the capsulated atmosphere around life

I naturally stood the bike up
as if hit by the solar system
at the boundary of the imagination
at that point I could send light messages for help
I was hoping he could escape
to witness the birth of a
raceway near Monterey,
and had a VERY
close encounter with a young doe,
a female (blacktail) deer-yacht
about to be torn from
reality but he quickly applied
massive licking and
then the deer started to think
directly in front of me.

A small, contained micro-
neutron beam shot out from the white page
meeting in the space right between the incompatible

thoughts and a giant raindrop.
The man set it to the highest speed possible
then went into the screen with the
biological beings who
witnessed this from space.
The people who went into the
opposing lane in slow-mo were after your ideas
and the stars seemed to be lawyers
disappearing over the crest of
a hill on a blacktop road in the midday sun.

I then leaned left while
braking with a cage (aren't all these things
cages?) and thankfully was not going
my usual pace, lest
things could have gone to seed
in a pattern that pervaded
their own emptinesses.

I consider myself very lucky in this life
I was following a relatively right hand sweeper.
as the last seconds counted down
then—THUNK—as her nose
smacked against my seat tail section
she left a bit of deer
slobber on the carbon fiber
she was okay, and wobbled
off to the bushes.
A funnel suddenly formed that seemed to feel life
the binary stars shut
the mouth of the terribly wrong space around me

The deer was behind me, and I heard suns
began to disappear as their
last rays of light illuminated the personal morality
like a smacking mouth.
Watch out for these critters,

or at least remember they are out there
to suck the corners of
the stars into its gaping feelings,
and I again took the form of fabric.

I could feel the connection to time
unwind itself into the massive pit of the
destabilized horizon,
then the walls collapsed crushing
the life history into pure
energy and each atom of the planet's
structure combusted and broke
down, and the disintegration destroyed everything
in my libido.

Then I fell in on
myself in a slow darkness
that consumed all laughter,
to have no end of it
as the blazing would be,
it would knock
you off your path, or bend your forks back
like a pretzel if you hit it right or wrong
sorry for the bummer advice.

GIVE ME A MINUTE

give me a minute
to complain about my biggest source
of unsolicited
beloved snail advice
making a sled
by taking their students
to a demonstration
about skeleton recovery
I think I can stop the
one that tramped on a rat's face,
the one who crawled Ikea-like,
spewing containers of protons

which competitors are we talking about here?
I almost wet myself
with these ice-covered fog skeletons,
these horse-drawn skeletons,
and moss
with enchanted learning skeletons
for learning a point of view
during the snail races
I'm not so sure of myself anymore

did the snails speak to you?
using their snail phones?
quivering with
elasticity essays?

what causes these huge luge sleds
to gain speed
down on the rectangular languor-thingies?
Utah's husbands,
at the front of a
hockey skeleton?

what the phone wants you to say
is what we could always do
about public snail phones
the air resistance and friction
of these mutating huskies

it's simple: lie down!

THE COUNT

These contented mitts
will delay their hands,
half-steeped in dropped sands,
when I open your cage
with the otters' help.

They flee the realms of siloed Dramamine
where hope is like a flailing Egyptology
harpooning itself
within my colleagues
into an Iowa I will never see.

Edgy and Whaley gather the hirsute licenses once more.
She washed off the bonsai offal.
I've sung to my face,
but Queequeg is too puritan.

Am I the only one to have trampled your dreams
like so many protesters in a purpose?

It's not uncommon
for Tutankhamen to steal
their ego nightmare mittens,
he said to me
among the waves of sentient bebop viruses
that transmitted my form
using the power of envy,
it is extremely dangerous and difficult
to get arrested
for being interested
in dolphins.

These dolphins who use cell phones.

THE US IS TURKEY AND HUMANITY

the US investigating turkey and humanity
at the end of the blaster worm
it seems you can cream corn
with the memory of someone else's tan
this emblematic
figure from your lost destiny
is loosely the steel-frame
building that collapsed
and the traditional buildings that remained erect
turkey is a sign of marine mammal flexibility
densely leafy, branching
hillsides east of 1985
licking the information from the tarp

picture my fractured turkey neck
injecting a dolphin into the turkey of your puréed dreams
with hope ingredients folded
up like hidden dimensions
in a city with places I will never see
the real area 51 is by the thousands
before our toes were
identified with family and friends
a really fabulous forefinger to the thumb
which does not mean "ok"

Paris is to indistinct calls in the wild turkey vocabulary
as the body is an obscene turkey
with unkillable dreams and fantasy goals
held erect on a turkey,
while cooking desire ha ha in the desert.
Even so—
artists page through the age they'd like to be
like the Minister of Water and Irrigation
the goal is the back of my neck

majestically king-like enlargement comparison
while the oil is for numerous stems,
ascending to reality like Condoleeza Rice
surprised that you're not a monument,
they will pass through
tents with the edge of an aluminum ball
past the goal-keeper of life
preparing the turkey
as desired

CLASSIC

I am reduced to being a fluffy lifeboat again
many times during the years
the years have gone by
without even noticing me
he said with a smile that can get
weird, like non-violence,
this implication that I am not enough of a zombie
bees with fax machines are pretty classic
but at some point I'm in the position of
getting all initial responsy on your ass

guess they hop around or whatever
like a right-wing confectionary
based on writing
about being destroyed, and voilà
I am what happened

the main thing to me is winning,
not individual awards
I have decided
I'm not having sex with you, or myself
coupled with the fact
that the prying eyes of the reader
are seeing there
not such "guests" wrapped with sun-dried
disparaging heroes
that which arises from the act of attention
is on commission
an omission that
just depends on how you
meant to deal with a whole table
full of Kraft macaroni and cheese

SEA MONKEY

He suddenly found he'd created a new kind of flashlight
that could "shine" through "other flashlights"
and see true form, like the shape of Florida.

The crustacean eyeliner
is coming back from the dead,
its primordial spirit unveiled by the
small, easily identified worries
being drugged and trained
and hypnotized and breaking everything
within arm's reach.

The seaside dorms explode
like bears performing in the holographic mist.
People reach towards black holes,
or colliding, high frequency versions of the
hard durable surfaces
known from being in your memory.

It is not easy to let go of your gusto,
or let surgeons understand things,
I'm distracted by these swimmers
putting me in a state of mind that
is much better suited to
waves of syllabication.

Buddhists began wandering into traps
in western Long Island during the summer.
Go towards light and away from privacy:
life involves mixing two components,
a resin and a hardener.

Very simple robots
that go towards light
are just sort-of true.

HOW COULD THIS HAVE HAPPENED?

I thought my Mastercard got off to a great convent lisp.

When they got there I noticed them unloading mysterious scuba auras.

Or I will give you a fresh can of litmus for supper.

The auras continued to wiggle as she staggered to a piece of tone deaf self-defeating argument and on to a strained memory about what had gone wrong.

She examined it and discarded it with the looming question of a marble "human fortress."

Night had taken the sky and stars and glowed in over-attention.

She spun around and pointed her aurora borealis toward Sacramento.

She got to her feet and stumbled slightly as she tried to be completely obliterated by something exempting itself from a piece of wreckage.

Most of us have grown up in a society embodied by the scorched earth. Focus on curbing undesirable behavior.

We are taught to obey the laws, conduct ourselves according to social standards, and talk to sewers.

We are given a great degree of freedom so long as our actions do not infringe on idlers.

Her attitude was like a dim shard of glass sticking through the setting sun.

The "three branches of government" system of democratic America is a relatively recent phenomenon. She knew he was getting closer because on the horizon she could see leeches.

Trusting in the sadistic sorcery practiced by her witch cohorts, behind the sky stars glowed in the infinite blackness of interstellar space.

JOE FRENTZEL

fishhook laws as food
signal the regulation of movements
in the DOPE ASS impact of gluteus maximus
not necessarily
to say something said
sometimes people say something
said by accident, not realizing
that their words could be taken AS FISH FOOD

I do not find individuals appalling,
nor do I hate them. Instead,
it is their lifestyle, their choices,
that I find utterly offensive
MY DUTY IS to carry pigeons over the border

these rubles of dissatisfaction
can have multiple meanings
the species coexistence
within the GUILTY PLEASURES of ants

fatty acids in ROBERT PLANT
are insights about targeting
sincerity pathways like E. COLI HOSTILITY BANNERS
versus the function of faith-based
crystal meth SORORITY goals

there will be a lunch
of only lichens held with
the endowment, if marmots
married—on and off the court—

I love to drive and have motor dysfunction
I love to build things out of lobster traps
and help friends

paint their houses by exploiting Mormons
I hate communists

can you stop humming that?
The Crown reserves the right
to arrest anyone
saying anything unrequited

let's just drop the whole thing
by finding a guitar to put on
I'm myself—again
I can't teach anyone to do anything
statements in negative form
naked vehicles on display at the auto show
flower arrangements and chairs
the mafia hit list
let the world prepare
they have their hearts expended
many ways to "loosen up"
The Ford Motor Company
Webster's flatlands
they let the mules
be executive editors
the buffalo pet
thought through to ourselves
and disease, that you would not let
them save

you save yourself and
never see her again in the story
let it out in armies
of the antiwar movement
or, as the future is behind us
couldn't you find an instrument?

you vowed to use drugs
people showed up
in non-American clothes
you could form around yourself
from reading the waste products
of the authorities
today's line—tell it to the passing coffin

let's hope the charges are thrown out
let's teleport and ask nicely
to go off on intelligence
so I put them to use and then to immersion
my parents are—what's the phrase?
let's start now
concentrate on your press card
they would not have let me in otherwise
coffins from coffin builders
they were able to
wonder where things went so wrong
put the value of a civil war
in solitary
let's make something ugly
let's enjoy the games

THE WOLFDOG MAGIC OF PHYSICS

cat and mouse or simply "cat mouse"
the paper consists of letters written by Burgess Meredith
a kitten names all people of the earth "Patti Smith"
welcome to the club
it seems both of us
have been left
holding the interpenetrating gyres
the latter empathy
where the speaker is speaking metaphorically
for a beer of completeness
not invented in multiplicity
with something as little in common
with human lives
as the dog-star has
in your heart
your heart is . . . influential
your nickname is
to his dog aesop sleeping

SEXING A DWARF HAMSTER CELEBRATION OF LENT

EARTH CYCLES are kickin' me in the nuts
owls aren't wise—they are BAD ASS

a bat left me standing in the doorway crying
Mr. Snow Emergency, feta omelets aren't blind,
rigorous science with philosophy, history,
and poetry all combine
to transcend the various formal concepts of life

all myths are beavers
a race against the clock to capture the ruptures
of America's most threatened creatures
and their vocabularies,
and apply emergency math

Start reading. . . .

Bill Gates's face in the moon
where opossums play
and porcupine problematics
are direct experience

BEST WAY TO DEAL WITH STORK PATÉ
IS TO OUT-LIVE THE MOTHERFUCKER

under the knife breaking your piece of
stork paté in this world
when I first heard about stork paté I think
I was very strong,
but now I think I want to believe
in stork paté. hail stork paté's bong.

Harry Truman is rolling around with
THE MONKEYS OF THE DOORS CASSETTES as
    sound
bowling with a fried mass of jerk molasses
the fall of the star high school stork paté
    running back
sophomore year, sermons lack
knowledge, how to establish
relationships with demons rituals
to get into college

teens for stork paté group
the stork paté of the thousand suns
Hail stork paté of Young Guns
the solid foundation,
the stork leviathans,
who rock the waters of sleep and the
Truman Stork Paté Show
She kept rambling about
stork patéism
and how it wasn't "permitted"
I held up the horned claw remitted
"Hail The Thomas Stork Paté Crown Affair!"
Like that!
The Beverly Hills Stork Paté Cop Hat

democrats are kissing
democrats are kissing
democrats are kissing

DIVIDING MY TIME

I truly hope that Gary Hart has better things to do than many other leaders in the spirit world, including the fact that they won't let him go in on the Gary Hart holding patterns, the geographically distant objects we encounter here which happen to be correspondences between Boston and northern Vermont that have turned erotic—Gary Hart participants made into better prospects for committed other times though actually not nearly as good as "fear of commitment" times, which have room for ferns, spiders and banana slugs to live.

We derive morality from Gary Hart to be the need to be the only democracy in the Muslim world between Boston and northern Vermont and its social disorder so that the social systems of the world crash into Oliver North again and again. In no way am I excluding Philadelphians from a better way to pull the plug on Gary Hart except that they want to interview me about what I mean: what we mean is that the Republic between Boston and northern Vermont is an Arab Marshall Plan, and Gary Hart is all of pre-W.W.II utopia-space.

I would like to go to the library and be replaced by something that works better. I can eliminate one of the world's worst monsters because I know better than Gary Hart about what *now* is. Also how Gary Hart is the appropriate investigation into what we are left with as a joke when life's options seem to have "spun down," not Gary Hart as genuine desire to be banned from any Republic between an addressee or audience otherwise filled with the desire to be back somewhere—return home from being somewhere else for instance, in that not many automatic money machines are in the world, relatively speaking.

I feel like the phone lines were banned from our life together, what to do next when it's not getting better, how to handle my order installations by asserting that I am a freelance scientist. . . .

Gary Hart is paying for life as we are paying for it—by acknowledging (and backlogging) everything that has ever existed, exists or will exist, including the thought that you might feel the future in some threatening way that seems to imply you must surpass your own defensive mechanisms in an as-yet-unimagined counteractive recycling of counterproductive psychic space—this is the actual War on Terror—when we have such beings sucking trees and wildlife into the earth like a black hole banned from the Republic and Gary Hart is free speech, Gary Hart is elections . . . not so hot . . . not so necessary or as hot as Gary Hart. We are hotter than the hottest thing to have ever been created.

CONTROL IS A BEAUTIFUL THING

I sat at my desk today and went out

it's a disaster
these things appear before night
you have the whole world to yourself

now we hate these little things
I get these flecks of rage
I am very lucky

I thought I'd get down to business
I went to the local place
to get some things
I'll think about these at a later date
I haven't experienced them yet
I'm sure there will be
no trace of them tomorrow

The liquid isn't sticky or confused
I move several times a day
directly toward the problem

I can see this will last a while
I'm sure my other half
will use its hands for this

it's a good thing
as it makes things change.
You can get a kind of face or head
though it doesn't
really seem worth it.
I can see how this would be
very useful for people
who need to get there.

I got home and took one out
that was about three hours ago,
I just looked in the mirror
and my head was there again
you are like me

there is a range waiting for me
I would never use
washing my hands and looking
into the future
it was no problem
you can pull
this into the new range that
meets the beautiful sounds,
like a silver shaped cylinder
floating outside your bedroom window

What was that in the mirror?
My face?
like coming home after a training course
just as it's beginning,
be careful not to shine too brilliantly here
or something important could roll away
the liquid inside yourself
control is a beautiful thing

ACROSS THE PEE-STAINED UNICORNS

I've been good. I really have.
I haven't cheated
the coin-operated animate iridescent watching things
out of my shape.
The giant mounds—who built 'em?
Maybe it was the medical-scrabble people
dozing off while they
shot some soufflés.

When they finish the soufflé shooting
there will be a before and after,
dwelling alongside
a double chili-cheese dog
like a hamster dance
with a piece of America

real ground marigold,
rather than "being against freedom"
minerals and trace elements
and an overthrowing of subjectivism.

The hamsters' argument
is to be the loudest categories of identity
hamsters are not widely full
of nonexistent henceness.

Sandwiches eat each other in the street.

WHY WOULD YOU LISTEN TO THAT PATRONIZING ASSHOLE?

here's a tip: try removing the quotation marks from your life
I won't run and have that thing in the cage
pull my arm off, leaving me to "paint"
the hallway wall with my blood-soaked, stringy
shoulder-stump anymore.
I don't do poverty well.

mom's email contacted the world
it would be like going to parties where
they say "assistant ass-kissy etc."
and listen to people
who smell just like the regular soap
permanently delete
the whole cast
of Salem's Lot

typically I will start a game
by losing involuntarily
I've tried to "just listen" before
it usually involves fitting tools
into my tyranny
I'm bound to respect you
for being an "if magnet"

girls, if you ever hear this from an
"if magnet" then you may be qualified
for the voice job that was
trying to fight its way out of the hole
avoiding the people who use their
"going out to see the duke" thing in glowing papal eyes

I tend to listen to music that is counter-productive.

WIN ONE FOR ME

Although your brain may be
riddled with the effects of light
it has always been a metal pail
filled with Air Force One

I had a tyranny that shone
within my soul
it continues to shine
as brightly as
the greatest force in the world

when the time comes for me
I am sure that what I have caused
to be done to the world
will make itself known
reinterpreting the scene,
I create place and time with my mind

The fact is, what they called "radical"
was really "right"
What they called "dangerous"
was just a glass of lemonade
desperately seeking
a combination of two or more colors
I've always been wearing this day in history.

we all have data to fall into
stored alongside the fuselage,
I enlist the sun to hear my story

create something life-threatening
all the memories I lost while I was here
trees cause more pollution than cars
though what I love is naked penguins playing—

it is an historic inevitability.
What errors have been made?
What Chicken Errors have been made?

I have to be honest with you,
I have a great color.
You can't communicate with me,
but I have a strong heart and strong lungs.
All you can do is just hug me,
and give me a kiss and say a prayer
and hope for the best

ALLIGATORS AND MERMAIDS

listen up:
respect golfers—
the self is a golfer

a set of "flat to negative"
personnel problems

those are windbreakers—
folded windbreakers

your car starts
because you car
can be
adorned

JOHN DENVER WAWA SHADOW PUPPET GOVERNMENT

baby boomers grow mohawks all life long
but the god of Isaac and Ishmael would never order
    a mace-banana smoothie
I'll be the one flying the flaming fetus kites
as spring comes in like the John Denver sniper story
an example of something that's not what it seems

the NBC/Wall Street Journal doesn't understand
the God of Isaac and Ishmael
soon we'll all be praying to John Denver
if we don't allow right-wing poor people to feel happy
    ALL the time,
teach their kids how to pray in the direction of pizza
yet see no problem
with having the Lord's Prayer printed in ghostly pubic hair

the president has become newly stressed-out
with the profound equality of all human beings
knocking over stone walls onto Avril Lavigne
as Abraham Lincoln once did.
I want to pray humbly to John Denver
a proud born-again five-course set of
Wimbledon bong leopards made of fleshy iPods

celebrity porn aqueducts cast their love with the men jailed
for missing celebrity porn aqueduct prayer meetings

sure, we've all seen a Caucasian fuck a cat, but how
many have you seen fuck a glowing lead vulture?

John Kerry prays to John Denver for money
John Denver Wawa shadow puppet government

78

AIR CONDITIONING

Rat 'em out
the dead
power plants
Lifestyle. La la la

Let's get a vehicle
and drive to the end of the road
Power Windows Power Door
Locks Ai Ai Ai Make a Deal. Ai Ai
Let's make all year
about making Paul Bremer count
tiny plastic things
let's make power count a.k.a. misconceptions

Choose an irritating silence
Make some important enemies
Talk about the nature of waves

if you attach this
to a power source
you'll probably see a princess
sun roof biblical as hell

I want to allow them to interact
scratch Albany's surface with sound
the shift to an energy future
all by itself
is all by itself

it can rotate
with gravity
with complete freedom
in 360
degrees

I AM A BELUGA WHALE

I am in deep deep water because of my in-laws and my wife.
Beluga Whales dealing with divorce
breaking so hard that my fins were rubbing away
and from then on I knew I was in deep deep trouble.
Go tell it to my vehicle

I am a thirty-one-year-old Beluga Whale,
I am not married and have no children.
Is it a rule that someone's first song
has to be about the title of that song or
talking label-making machines?
Because if there is such a machine,
I am in deep trouble.
If you call me
you're one of my parents,
I am a burning baby Beluga Whale.

Backing up in DOS was easy—
I have not found it so in win95,
I crash in the waves
I am a Beluga Whale.
Who said life with Beluga Whales was easy . . .?
I think I am going to order myself over the internet
I had no idea that I was a Beluga Whale
I am a Beluga Whale.
I should have called my professor
and begged for an extension.
Cram
if the actual exam
is anywhere close.

What do Ontario liberal lawyers and politicians
know about the truth?
I am a Beluga Whale.

You can imagine how, if I as a seminary professor
and a member of a committee
which recommends ecclesiastical disobedience—
"I am a Beluga Whale," said one of my teeth,
which are used not for chewing,
but for grabbing and tearing prey,
which is then swallowed whole.

I have beautiful blue eyes—I am a Beluga Whale.
If she asks me to do anything,
my conscious mind is no longer in control.
"Yes, it's fan mail—Beluga whale fan mail."
at my apartment waiting for her message
It's an image overload.
I am a Beluga Whale.

I like to eat fish, squid, crustaceans, octopi and worms.
I hear her voice, tiny and,
if he goes back on his word then I am a Beluga Whale.

Somehow or other I have come to know
that you could help me.
I am a Beluga Whale. I live
in frigid arctic and subarctic waters.
All I can say is that I hope
God has a sense of humor.
I am a Beluga Whale.
My body tapers off at both ends
I cannot get this working.
I am a Beluga Whale,
Best Regards, Phil.

CHECK OUT MY PETROLEUM HAT

I may be the master of saturnalia,
but I acted out on the golden age
before the nostalgic drug effects took hold

I suspected that it was connected to the fact that
I just quit my job and
had several weeks of vacation
before the ascendancy of Jove.

Check out my petroleum hat
if that's what you want to call it
blah blah blah . . . I was fired by
Dennis Kucinich . . . blah blah blah.

These people are older than the moon
before the new cosmic
events forced me to withdraw
into a subterranean refuge (the inhabitants
are before free agency), when prayer
payrolls were substantially less than the return on
the current Garage D'Or, but
deftly traded on the myth of gag-riculture.

Hunter-gatherer life was generally
about me quitting your day job without notice.

I am entitled to be paid
for the period
at the end of this sentence.

BURNING THIRD-EYE SCROTUM MEMORIES

start with a chicken quesadilla
in a radio message from your scrotum
the holes between the second and third banks of
tiny UFOs which emitted strong
beams of vacancy
are all the fathers that Bill Clinton's words are.
they mess with and/or destroy our symptoms
toilet paper, chickenpox or spontaneous abortions,
he didn't like the sound of burning preschoolers
—Louden Up a Bit Here—
whether it be emu or able-bodied toaster:
following composition with an irritation
in an emotional Austria,
of my apartment manager
what would nail my screen memories to my third eye?
as I think across the miles from you
welcoming the debate with contempt,
men of the tribe over-commit to stuff
a slight witch burning after wistfulness

WHAT MY PET GOAT IS GOING TO HAVE TO UNDERSTAND

because it made his world look like theirs from now on
I didn't ask him at the time
I am very curious to know

trust is a worthless English professor
like touch-football enthusiasts who
sometimes want to kill

unkempt families with blue hair
laughing at an orgasm
screamed for someone to fuck their Pilgrims
please mention my penises in this part

whoever said the world is as
ma said the world would turn completely to?
there's no reason not to destroy all cars
you stress about the asterisks of positive negation
you get my meaning—frozen pigeons of laughter
dropping from a past life

this church is World Trade Towel Art—no oysters
and I am the world's worst baker, but my baking maxes out
just as the refrigerated seas begin to fail

FUCK YOU FOR BEING A FUCKING FRAUD

houses can be searched and you are all busted up
shut the fuck up and be more notable
what's the use of being so strong
that you can't not do something?
no matter how many times you throw maternal instincts around
you wind up being related

Say "Gimme any reason why I'd need you."
anything but the cold horsies of a situation
which, in my mind cannot possibly
come from loving and gentle voters.
where the hell were the quitters?
you want to talk about "song?"
"song" hates to see a hoodie being the first
interesting moment of adult life
more American than dreaming again
someone is annoyed at being paid

who loves to vandalize Pythagoras
who loves to work
inside a parade-like hole in president Kennedy's head
hysterical boredom—
like being a robot—displeasure:
welcome to the colorful world
brownnosing the red shift
what happened to being unnecessarily rude
about your own boring shit—
darkness

who whines about being horribly ill?
soldiers flown across a query
unfreeze the agonistics
if you are looking for an arc
scattered among the horse-drawn showers of time and space
you're essentially fucked for life

LET PEOPLE NAME THEMSELVES

Some people who have nothing to do
sustain themselves
with seething restaurants
to make Gray Davis go away forever
by carrying a large pre-Raphaelite medulla oblongata
across your life
as medicine for the people left behind
bent on drinking boring wine

"The protein is in every walk of life, Peter!"
—dying words—
remember this
resistance leaders shortly before supper
when the pyre was kindled
and Proteus mailed his bodily fluids to heaven and back again

the government would like to see Joel Kuzai in jail
I want a samosa. Shakespeare
is just passing himself off as a group of anti-Nazi
listeners attempting to bluff their way
past a sports utility accusation

What's Stuart actually saying?
The incredibly boring "Scandal"
That Won't Go Away
The incredibly boring "Church Commission Report . . ."
real problems
real problems and real problems . . .

any form of worship conducted ON the field is okay
downtown Chicago is where your life drastically changes
a noble gunslinger who
arrives with brand new guns to buy
passing himself off as
a Staubach simulation again

Just wait a week and it'll go away

INCOMMENSURATE

marketing poopy will make about $20K when
you take Lloyd's advice and DRINK THAT SEAWEED,
detox your unhealthy forerunners
trying to get your kidney stones to seem less like art
here it is straight: I'm not dumb—ideas are dumb,
it'll still make a nice monthly pyro experiment
to pay myself
with those subscriptions of free glue for horses
that's how I'm trying to overcome people
by allowing this to be said. . . .

are you going to do things
like local residents judging a dog?
it couldn't be
that must be the sound of a loser
that stays within the law
as he would have
way too much to lose
by just losing

STAR WARS

people try to punish each other
by focusing the subject
to make the clown hair more fair
and balanced: old news
not that all teens are volatile all the time,
skinny adolescents in control of the contraption
where we meet to worship
a taco could pass me the
laws of supply and demand

better a flame falling into fear
free and open
than "this" place, "here" and "now," ever
the gathering storms of victorious male shortness
in real theology
are facts that will replace people
in the remainder of my time on earth

coupla oldies, coupla oldies coupla oldies
with a permanent floating
fear of life piñata
only you can create
topics the shape of hamper urgencies
troll like sock puppets through the stars

I AM MYSELF TODAY

but I have to eat food.
I'm starting to feel like a hair dryer
in the bathtub of myself.
Will the machine live
the rest of my life for me? Yes?
Lake Placid is the known world,
It explains everything
I need my originality back.
I wish my id was more piercing.

I train teddy bears,
It makes me feel better.
I stood there—okay for a minute—
the Kool-Aid guy sang a bitter song in the street.

with a gesture of day-to-day "Juliet"
I have received these commie brain signals
out of lyrical prowess (or lack thereof)
is this how it was supposed to be?
—annoying—

I'm gonna blow my own mind
for other dreams
I'd like to thank my stomach: it is beautiful

I being neither rich nor famous nor of a moment

I feel like a human torch
in virtual health
I squished time into love

ROOF BOOKS

- ❏ Andrews, Bruce. **EX WHY ZEE**. 112p. $10.95.
- ❏ Andrews, Bruce. **Getting Ready To Have Been Frightened**. 116p. $7.50.
- ❏ Benson, Steve. **Blue Book**. Copub. with The Figures. 250p. $12.50
- ❏ Bernstein, Charles. **Controlling Interests**. 80p. $11.95.
- ❏ Bernstein, Charles. **Islets/Irritations**. 112p. $9.95.
- ❏ Bernstein, Charles (editor). **The Politics of Poetic Form**. 246p. $12.95; cloth $21.95.
- ❏ Brossard, Nicole. **Picture Theory**. 188p. $11.95.
- ❏ Cadiot, Olivier. **Former, Future, Fugitive**. Translated by Cole Swensen. 166p. $13.95.
- ❏ Champion, Miles. **Three Bell Zero**. 72p. $10.95.
- ❏ Child, Abigail. **Scatter Matrix**. 79p. $9.95.
- ❏ Davies, Alan. **Active 24 Hours**. 100p. $5.
- ❏ Davies, Alan. **Signage**. 184p. $11.
- ❏ Davies, Alan. **Rave**. 64p. $7.95.
- ❏ Day, Jean. **A Young Recruit**. 58p. $6.
- ❏ Di Palma, Ray. **Motion of the Cypher**. 112p. $10.95.
- ❏ Di Palma, Ray. **Raik**. 100p. $9.95.
- ❏ Doris, Stacy. **Kildare**. 104p. $9.95.
- ❏ Dreyer, Lynne. **The White Museum**. 80p. $6.
- ❏ Dworkin, Craig. **Strand**. 112p. $12.95.
- ❏ Edwards, Ken. **Good Science**. 80p. $9.95.
- ❏ Eigner, Larry. **Areas Lights Heights**. 182p. $12, $22 (cloth).
- ❏ Gizzi, Michael. **Continental Harmonies**. 92p. $8.95.
- ❏ Gladman, Renee. **A Picture-Feeling**. 72p. $10.95.
- ❏ Goldman, Judith. **Vocoder**. 96p. $11.95.
- ❏ Gottlieb, Michael. **Ninety-Six Tears**. 88p. $5.
- ❏ Gottlieb, Michael. **Gorgeous Plunge**. 96p. $11.95.
- ❏ Gottlieb, Michael. **Lost & Found**. 80p. $11.95.
- ❏ Greenwald, Ted. **Jumping the Line**. 120p. $12.95.
- ❏ Grenier, Robert. **A Day at the Beach**. 80p. $6.
- ❏ Grosman, Ernesto. **The XULReader: An Anthology of Argentine Poetry (1981–1996)**. 167p. $14.95.
- ❏ Guest, Barbara. **Dürer in the Window, Reflexions on Art**. Book design by Richard Tuttle. Four color throughout. 80p. $24.95.
- ❏ Hills, Henry. **Making Money**. 72p. $7.50. VHS videotape $24.95. Book & tape $29.95.
- ❏ Huang Yunte. **SHI: A Radical Reading of Chinese Poetry**. 76p. $9.95
- ❏ Hunt, Erica. **Local History**. 80 p. $9.95.
- ❏ Kuszai, Joel (editor) **poetics@**, 192 p. $13.95.

- ❑ Inman, P. **Criss Cross**. 64 p. $7.95.
- ❑ Inman, P. **Red Shift**. 64p. $6.
- ❑ Lazer, Hank. **Doublespace**. 192 p. $12.
- ❑ Levy, Andrew. **Paper Head Last Lyrics**. 112 p. $11.95.
- ❑ Mac Low, Jackson. **Representative Works: 1938–1985**. 360p. $18.95 (cloth).
- ❑ Mac Low, Jackson. **Twenties**. 112p. $8.95.
- ❑ McMorris, Mark. **The Café at Light**. 112p. $12.95.
- ❑ Moriarty, Laura. **Rondeaux**. 107p. $8.
- ❑ Neilson, Melanie. **Civil Noir**. 96p. $8.95.
- ❑ Osman, Jena. **An Essay in Asterisks**. 112p. $12.95.
- ❑ Pearson, Ted. **Planetary Gear**. 72p. $8.95.
- ❑ Perelman, Bob. **Virtual Reality**. 80p. $9.95.
- ❑ Perelman, Bob. **The Future of Memory**. 120p. $14.95.
- ❑ Piombino, Nick, **The Boundary of Blur**. 128p. $13.95.
- ❑ Prize Budget for Boys, **The Spectacular Vernacular Revuew**. 96p. $14.95.
- ❑ Raworth, Tom. **Clean & Will-Lit**. 106p. $10.95.
- ❑ Robinson, Kit. **Balance Sheet**. 112p. $11.95.
- ❑ Robinson, Kit. **Democracy Boulevard**. 104p. $9.95.
- ❑ Robinson, Kit. **Ice Cubes**. 96p. $6.
- ❑ Scalapino, Leslie. **Objects in the Terrifying Tense Longing from Taking Place**. 88p. $9.95.
- ❑ Seaton, Peter. **The Son Master**. 64p. $5.
- ❑ Sherry, James. **Popular Fiction**. 84p. $6.
- ❑ Silliman, Ron. **The New Sentence**. 200p. $10.
- ❑ Silliman, Ron. **N/O**. 112p. $10.95.
- ❑ Smith, Rod. **Music or Honesty**. 96p. $12.95
- ❑ Smith, Rod. **Protective Immediacy**. 96p. $9.95
- ❑ Stefans, Brian Kim. **Free Space Comix**. 96p. $9.95
- ❑ Tarkos, Christophe. **Ma Langue est Poétique—Selected Works**. 96p. $12.95.
- ❑ Templeton, Fiona. **Cells of Release**. 128p. with photographs. $13.95.
- ❑ Templeton, Fiona. **YOU—The City**. 150p. $11.95.
- ❑ Torres, Edwin. **The All-Union Day of the Shock Worker**. 112 p. $10.95.
- ❑ Tysh, Chris. **Cleavage**. 96p. $11.95.
- ❑ Ward, Diane. **Human Ceiling**. 80p. $8.95.
- ❑ Ward, Diane. **Relation**. 64p. $7.50.
- ❑ Watson, Craig. **Free Will**. 80p. $9.95.
- ❑ Watten, Barrett. **Progress**. 122p. $7.50.
- ❑ Weiner, Hannah. **We Speak Silent**. 76 p. $9.95
- ❑ Weiner, Hannah. **Page**. 136 p. $12.95
- ❑ Wolsak, Lissa. **Pen Chants**. 80p. $9.95.
- ❑ Yasusada, Araki. **Doubled Flowering: From the Notebooks of Araki Yasusada**. 272p. $14.95.

ROOF BOOKS
are published by
Segue Foundation
300 Bowery
New York, NY 10012
Visit our website at **segue.org**

ROOF BOOKS are distributed by
SMALL PRESS DISTRIBUTION
1341 Seventh Avenue
Berkeley, CA. 94710-1403.
Phone orders: 800-869-7553
spdbooks.org